My Bilingual Picture Book

كتابي المصور ثنائي اللغة

Sefa's most beautiful children's stories in one volume

Ulrich Renz • Barbara Brinkmann:

Sleep Tight, Little Wolf · نَمْ جيداً، أيُها الذئبُ الصغيرْ

For ages 2 and up

Cornelia Haas • Ulrich Renz:

My Most Beautiful Dream · أَسْعَدُ أَحْلَامِي

For ages 2 and up

Ulrich Renz • Marc Robitzky:

The Wild Swans · البجع البري

Based on a fairy tale by Hans Christian Andersen

For ages 5 and up

© 2024 by Sefa Verlag Kirsten Bödeker, Lübeck, Germany. www.sefa-verlag.de

Special thanks to Paul Bödeker, Freiburg, Germany

All rights reserved.

ISBN: 9783756304257

Read · Listen · Understand

Translation:

Pete Savill (English)

Abdelaaziz Boussayer (Arabic)

Audiobook and video:

www.sefa-bilingual.com/bonus

Password for free access:

English: **LWEN1423**

Arabic: **LWAR1027**

Good night, Tim! We'll continue searching tomorrow.
Now sleep tight!

ليلة سعيدة يا تيم!

غداً سَنُتابعُ البحث. أما الآنْ فنمْ جيدا!

It is already dark outside.

لقد حلَّ الظلام.

What is Tim doing?

ماذا يَفعلُ تيم هُناك؟

He is leaving for the playground.

What is he looking for there?

إنه خارِجٌ إلى الملعب.
عَنْ ماذا يبحَثُ هُناك؟

The little wolf!

He can't sleep without it.

عَنْ الذئب الصغير!

لأنه لا يستطيع النومَ بدونه.

Who's this coming?

مَنْ القَادِم؟

Marie! She's looking for her ball.

إنها ماري! تبحث عن كُرَتِها.

And what is Tobi looking for?

و عَنْ ماذا يَبحَثُ طوبي؟

His digger.

عن حَفَّارَتِهِ.

And what is Nala looking for?

و عَنْ ماذا تَبَحَثُ نالا؟

Her doll.

عن دُميتِها.

Don't the children have to go to bed?
The cat is rather surprised.

ألم يَحِنْ وقتْ نَومِ الأطفال؟
تَتَساءَلُ القطة بعجب.

Who's coming now?

مَن القَادِم الآن؟

Tim's mum and dad!

They can't sleep without their Tim.

أمُ تيم و أبوه!

فهم لا يَستَطِيعونَ النَّومَ بدونِ ابنِهما تيم.

More of them are coming! Marie's dad.
Tobi's grandpa. And Nala's mum.

و هنالك المزيدُ قادمون!
أبو ماري. جدُّ طوبي. و أمُ نالا.

Now hurry to bed everyone!

الآن أسرِعوا إلى النوم!

Good night, Tim!

Tomorrow we won't have to search any longer.

ليلة سعيدة يا تيم!

غداً لن يكونَ علينا البحثُ مجدداً.

Sleep tight, little wolf!

نَمْ جيداً، أيُها الذئبُ الصغيرْ!

Cornelia Haas • Ulrich Renz

My Most Beautiful Dream

أَسْعَدُ أَحْلَامِي

Translation:

Sefâ Jesse Konuk Agnew (English)

Oumaima Naffouti (Arabic)

Audiobook and video:

www.sefa-bilingual.com/bonus

Password for free access:

English: BDEN1423

Arabic: BDAR1027

My
Most Beautiful Dream

أَسْعَدُ أَحْلَامِي

Cornelia Haas · Ulrich Renz

English　　　bilingual　　　Arabic

Lulu can't fall asleep. Everyone else is dreaming already – the shark, the elephant, the little mouse, the dragon, the kangaroo, the knight, the monkey, the pilot. And the lion cub. Even the bear has trouble keeping his eyes open …

Hey bear, will you take me along into your dream?

لُولُو لَا تَسْتَطِيعُ النَّوْمَ، الآخَرُونَ فِي سُبَاتٍ عَمِيقٍ يَحْلُمُونَ؛ القِرْشُ، اَلْفِيلُ، الفَأْرَةُ الصَّغِيرَةُ، التِّنِّينُ، الْكُنْغُرُ، الفَارِسُ، اَلْقِرْدُ، الطَّيَّارُ وَاَلْشِبْلُ. حَتَّى الدُّبُّ الصَّغِيرُ يَفْتَحُ أَعيَنَهُ بِصُعوبَةٍ أَيُّهَا الدُّبُّ الصَّغيرُ!

هَلْ تَأْخُذُنِي مَعَكَ فِي حُلْمِكَ؟

And with that, Lulu finds herself in bear dreamland. The bear catches fish in Lake Tagayumi. And Lulu wonders, who could be living up there in the trees?

When the dream is over, Lulu wants to go on another adventure. Come along, let's visit the shark! What could he be dreaming?

وَفِي الْحَالِ هَاهِي لُولُو فِي بَلَدِ أَحْلَامِ الدِّبَبَةِ. كَانَ الدُّبُّ الصَّغِيرُ يَصْطَادُ الْأَسْمَاكَ فِي بُحَيْرَةِ تَاغَايُومِي وَلُولُو تَتَسَاءَلُ مَنْ يُمْكِنُهُ الْعَيْشَ فَوْقَ الْأَشْجَارِ.

عِنْدَمَا انْتَهَى الْحِلْمُ، لُولُو تُرِيدُ مُغَامَرَةً أُخْرَى. تَعَالَ مَعِي لِرُؤْيَةِ الْقِرْشِ، بِمَاذَا هُوَ حَالِمٌ؟

The shark plays tag with the fish. Finally he's got some friends! Nobody's afraid of his sharp teeth.

When the dream is over, Lulu wants to go on another adventure. Come along, let's visit the elephant! What could he be dreaming?

القِرْشُ يَلْعَبُ لِعْبَةَ الْمُطارَدَةِ مَعَ الْأَسْماكِ. أخيراً أصْبَحَ لَهُ أَصْدِقاءُ إِلا أَحَدَ يَخافُ أَسْنانَهُ الْمُذَبَّبَة.

عِنْدَما انْتَهَى الْحِلْمُ، لُولُو مازالَتْ تُريدُ مُغامَرَةً أُخْرَى. تَعالَيا مَعي لِرُؤْيَةِ الْفيلِ بِماذا هُوَ حالِمٌ؟

The elephant is as light as a feather and can fly! He's about to land on the celestial meadow.

When the dream is over, Lulu wants to go on another adventure. Come along, let's visit the little mouse! What could she be dreaming?

اَلْفِيلُ خَفِيفٌ مِثْلِ اَلرَّيْشَةِ وَيَسْتَطِيعُ الطَّيَرَانَ. وَهُوَ عَلى وَشَكِ أَنْ يَحُطَّ في المَرْجِ السَّمَوِيِّ. عِنْدَمَا انْتَهَى الحِلْمُ، لُولُو مَازَالَتْ تُرِيدُ مُغَامَرَةً أُخْرَى. تَعالَوْا مَعِي لِرُؤْيَةِ الفَأْرَةِ الصَّغِيرَةِ بِمَاذَا هِيَ حَالِمَةٌ؟

The little mouse watches the fair. She likes the roller coaster best.
When the dream is over, Lulu wants to go on another adventure. Come along, let's visit the dragon! What could she be dreaming?

الفَأْرَةُ الصَّغِيرَةُ تَزورُ مَدينَةَ المَلاهي. أَعْجَبَتْها لُعْبَةُ الأُفْعَوانَةِ كَثيراً.
عِنْدَما انْتَهى الحِلْمُ، لُولُو تُريدُ مُغامَرَةً جَديدَةً. تَعالَوْا مَعي لِرُؤْيَةِ التِّنّينِ بِماذا هوَ حالِمٌ؟

The dragon is thirsty from spitting fire. She'd like to drink up the whole lemonade lake.
When the dream is over, Lulu wants to go on another adventure. Come along, let's visit the kangaroo! What could she be dreaming?

التِّنِّينُ عَطْشانٌ لِأَنَّهُ يَنْفُثُ النَّارَ مِنْ فَمِهِ. يَتَمَنَّى شُرْبَ بُحَيْرَةِ عَصِيرِ اللَّيْمُونِ كامِلَةً. عِنْدَما انْتَهَى الحِلْمُ، لُولُو مازالَتْ تُرِيدُ مُغامَرَةً أُخْرَى. تَعالَوْا مَعِي نَزورَ الْكَنْغَرَ بِماذا هوَ حالِمٌ؟

The kangaroo jumps around the candy factory and fills her pouch. Even more of the blue sweets! And more lollipops! And chocolate!
When the dream is over, Lulu wants to go on another adventure. Come along, let's visit the knight! What could he be dreaming?

الْكُنْغَرُ يَقْفِزُ فِي مَصْنَعِ الحَلْوَى وَيَمْلَأُ جَيْبَهُ مَزِيدًا مِنْ هَذِهِ الحَلْوَى الزَّرْقَاءِ! مَزِيدًا مِنْ الْمَصَاصَاتِ! وَالشُّكْلَاطَةُ!

عِنْدَمَا انْتَهَى الحِلْمُ، لُولُو مَازَالَتْ تُرِيدُ مُغَامَرَةً أُخْرَى. تَعَالَوْا مَعِي لِرُؤْيَةِ الفَارِسِ بِمَاذَا هُوَ حَالِمٌ؟

The knight is having a cake fight with his dream princess. Oops! The whipped cream cake has gone the wrong way!
When the dream is over, Lulu wants to go on another adventure. Come along, let's visit the monkey! What could he be dreaming?

الفارِسُ يَخوضُ مَعْرَكَةَ المُرَطِّباتِ مَعَ أميرَةِ أَحْلامِهِ. يَا لِلْهَوْلِ! قِطْعَةُ المُرَطِّباتِ أَخْطَأَتْ الهَدَفَ!

عِنْدَمَا انْتَهَى الحِلْمُ، لُولُو مَازَالَتْ تُريدُ مُغامَرَةً أُخْرَى. تَعالَوْا مَعِي لِرُؤْيَةِ القِرْدِ بِمَاذَا هُوَ حالِمٌ؟

Snow has finally fallen in Monkeyland. The whole barrel of monkeys is beside itself and getting up to monkey business.
When the dream is over, Lulu wants to go on another adventure. Come along, let's visit the pilot! In which dream could he have landed?

تَساقطَ الثَّلجُ أخيرًا فِي أرْضِ القِرَدَةِ. فِرْقَةُ القِرَدَةِ خَرَجَتْ مِنْ دِيَارِهَا يَشْعُرُونَ بِالنَّشْوَةِ وَ يَتَصَرَّفُونَ مِثْلَ المَجانينِ، تُغْنِي وَتَرْقُصُ وَتَقُومُ بِحَماقاتٍ.

عِنْدَمَا اِنْتَهَى الحِلْمُ، لُولُو مَازَالَتْ تُرِيدُ مُغَامَرَةً أُخْرَى. تَعالُوا مَعِي لِرُؤْيَةِ الطَّيّارِ أَيْنَ رَسَى حُلْمَهُ؟

The pilot flies on and on. To the ends of the earth, and even farther, right on up to the stars. No other pilot has ever managed that.
When the dream is over, everybody is very tired and doesn't feel like going on many adventures anymore. But they'd still like to visit the lion cub.
What could she be dreaming?

الطَّيَّارُ يَطِيرُ وَيَطِيرُ حَتَّى نِهايَةِ العالَمِ وَأَكْثَرَ، حَتَّى النُّجومِ. لَمْ يَفْعَلْها حَتَّى طَيَّارٌ مِنْ قَبْلِهِ.
عِنْدَما انْتَهَى الحِلْمُ، كَانَ الكُلُّ مُتْعَبًا وَلَا يَرْغَبُونَ فِي مُغَامَراتٍ جَدِيدَةٍ لَكِنَّهُمْ يُرِيدُونَ زِيارَةَ
اَلشِّبْلِ بِمَاذَا هُوَ حَالِمٌ يَا تَرَى؟

The lion cub is homesick and wants to go back to the warm, cozy bed.
And so do the others.

And thus begins ...

اَلْشِبْلُ يَشْتَاقُ إِلَى دِيَارِهِ وَيُرِيدُ الرُّجوعَ لِفِرَاشِهِ الدَّافِئِ الحَنونِ.

والْآخَرونَ أَيْضًا.

وَهُنَا يَبْدَأُ...

... Lulu's
most beautiful dream.

... أَسْعَدُ أَحْلامِ لُولُو.

Ulrich Renz • Marc Robitzky

The Wild Swans
البجع البري

Translation:

Ludwig Blohm, Pete Savill (English)

Inana Othman, Seraa Haider (Arabic)

Audiobook and video:

www.sefa-bilingual.com/bonus

Password for free access:

English: **WSEN1423**

Arabic: **WSAR1027**

Ulrich Renz · Marc Robitzky

The Wild Swans
البجع البري

Based on a fairy tale by
Hans Christian Andersen

English   bilingual   Arabic

Once upon a time there were twelve royal children – eleven brothers and one older sister, Elisa. They lived happily in a beautiful castle.

كان ياما كان في سالف العصر والأوان، كان يوجد ملك لديه اثنى عشر إبناً وإبنة – أحد عشر أميراً وأختهم الكبرى، إليزا. كانوا يعيشون بسعادة في قصر جميل.

One day the mother died, and some time later the king married again. The new wife, however, was an evil witch. She turned the eleven princes into swans and sent them far away to a distant land beyond the large forest.

في يوم من الأيام ماتت الأم، وبعد مدة من الزمن تزوج الملك ثانيةً. الزوجة الجديدة للملك كانت ساحرة شريرة؛ فقد سحرت الأمراء الإثني عشر وحوّلتهم إلى بجع وأبعدتهم إلى بلاد نائية، محاطة بالغابات من كل جوانبها.

She dressed the girl in rags and smeared an ointment onto her face that turned her so ugly, that even her own father no longer recognized her and chased her out of the castle. Elisa ran into the dark forest.

أما الأميرة، فقد ألبستَها الملكة الساحرة رداءاً رثّاً ولطَّخت وجهها بصباغ قبيح، حتى أنَ أباها الملك لم يعد بمقدوره التعرف عليها، فقام بطردها من القصر. إليزا هربت راكضةً إلى الغابة المظلمة.

Now she was all alone, and longed for her missing brothers from the depths of her soul. As the evening came, she made herself a bed of moss under the trees.

أصبحت الأميرة، الآن، وحيدة تماماً وتشعر بشوق شديد من أعماق قلبها الى إخوتها المفقودين. وحين حلَ الليل صنعت الأميرة لنفسها سريراً من الأعشاب والأشنة تحت الاشجار.

The next morning she came to a calm lake and was shocked when she saw her reflection in it. But once she had washed, she was the most beautiful princess under the sun.

في صباح اليوم التالي واصلت الأميرة سيرها ووصلت إلى بحيرة هادئة، إلى أن ارتعبت حين رأت إنعكاس وجهها على سطح ماء البحيرة، فقامت بغسل وجهها، وعادت مرة اخرى أجمل أميرة تحت الشمس.

After many days Elisa reached the great sea. Eleven swan feathers were bobbing on the waves.

بمرور الأيام وصلت الأميرة إلى البحر الكبير، حيث كانت إحدى عشرة ريشة من ريش البجع تتأرجح على الأمواج.

As the sun set, there was a swooshing noise in the air and eleven wild swans landed on the water. Elisa immediately recognized her enchanted brothers. They spoke swan language and because of this she could not understand them.

أثناء غروب الشمس تناهت أصوات في الأجواء، وعلى أثرها هبط أحد عشر بجعاً برياً على الماء. على الفور أدركت إليزا أنهم أشقاؤها الأحد عشر. ولأنهم يتحدثون فقط لغة البجع، لم تستطع أن تفهم كلامهم.

During the day the swans flew away, and at night the siblings snuggled up together in a cave.

One night Elisa had a strange dream: Her mother told her how she could release her brothers from the spell. She should knit shirts from stinging nettles and throw one over each of the swans. Until then, however, she was not allowed to speak a word, or else her brothers would die.
Elisa set to work immediately. Although her hands were burning as if they were on fire, she carried on knitting tirelessly.

أثناء النهار كان البجع يطير بعيداً، وليلاً يحتضن الأخوة بعضهم بعضاً في الكهف.

في إحدى الليالي حلمت إليزا حلماً غريباً: رأت أمها تخبرها فيه، كيف تفكُّ السحر عن إخوتها، حيث يجب عليها أن تحيك قميصاً صغيراً من نبات القرّاص لكل بجعة، وأن تلق به عليها. لكن لا يتوجب عليها أن تنطق بكلمة واحدة، إلى أن تنهي المهمة؛ وإلّا فسيموت إخوتها.
على الفور بدأت إليزا بالعمل وعلى الرغم من لسعات نبات القرّاص الحارقة ليديها إلّا أنها واظبت على الحياكة دون كللٍ أو ملل.

One day hunting horns sounded in the distance. A prince came riding along with his entourage and he soon stood in front of her. As they looked into each other's eyes, they fell in love.

في أحد الأيام تناهت أصوات أبواق الصيد من البعيد إلى مسامعها. ظهر أمير بصحبة حاشيته، وعلى الفور أسرع الأمير إلى المثول أمامها. وبمجرد رؤيتهما لبعضهما وقعا في الحب.

The prince lifted Elisa onto his horse and rode to his castle with her.

قام الأمير بوضع إليزا على حصانه وتوجه بها إلى قصره.

The mighty treasurer was anything but pleased with the arrival of the silent beauty. His own daughter was meant to become the prince's bride.

وزير الخزانة القوي فور أن رأى البكماء الجميلة أصبح أبعد مايكون عن السعادة. إبنته كانت العروس المرتقبة للأمير.

Elisa had not forgotten her brothers. Every evening she continued working on the shirts. One night she went out to the cemetery to gather fresh nettles. While doing so she was secretly watched by the treasurer.

إليزا لم تنس إخوتها. مساء كل يوم كانت تقوم بمواصلة حياكة القمصان. في إحدى الليالي ذهبت إلى المقبرة لجلب بعض نبات القرّاص الطري وكان وزير الخزانة يراقبها سراً.

As soon as the prince was away on a hunting trip, the treasurer had Elisa thrown into the dungeon. He claimed that she was a witch who met with other witches at night.

وحين كان الأمير في إحدى رحلات الصّيد، رمى وزير الخزانة إليزا في السجن. حيث ادّعى بأنها ساحرة شريرة تلتقي ليلاً بساحرات أخريات.

At dawn, Elisa was fetched by the guards. She was going to be burned to death at the marketplace.

وفي مطلع الفجر أقتيدت إليزا من قبل الحراس كي يتم إحراقها في ساحة المدينة.

No sooner had she arrived there, when suddenly eleven white swans came flying towards her. Elisa quickly threw a shirt over each of them. Shortly thereafter all her brothers stood before her in human form. Only the smallest, whose shirt had not been quite finished, still had a wing in place of one arm.

وبمجرد أن وصلت إليزا هناك، حتى حامت فجأة إحدى عشرة بجعة بريّة بيضاء. وبسرعة رمت إليزا على كل واحدة منها قميصاً معمولاً من نبات القرّاص. وعلى الفور وقف إخوتها أمامها على هيأتهم البشرية. فقط الأخ الأصغر، لم يكن قميصه قد أكتمل تماماً، فبقيت إحدى ذراعيه جناحاً.

The siblings' joyous hugging and kissing hadn't yet finished as the prince returned. At last Elisa could explain everything to him. The prince had the evil treasurer thrown into the dungeon. And after that the wedding was celebrated for seven days.

And they all lived happily ever after.

تواصلت القبلات والأشواق بين الإخوة حتى بعد عودة الأمير. وأخيراً استطاعت إليزا أن تسرد للأمير كل حكايتها. ألقي الأمير الوزير الشرير في السجن، واستمرت الأفراح والليالي الملاح طوال سبعة أيام.

ولو لم يكن الموت قدراً محتوماً لكانوا عاشوا إلى يومنا هذا.

Hans Christian Andersen

Hans Christian Andersen was born in the Danish city of Odense in 1805, and died in 1875 in Copenhagen. He gained world fame with his literary fairy-tales such as „The Little Mermaid", „The Emperor's New Clothes" and „The Ugly Duckling". The tale at hand, „The Wild Swans", was first published in 1838. It has been translated into more than one hundred languages and adapted for a wide range of media including theater, film and musical.

Barbara Brinkmann was born in Munich in 1969 and grew up in the foothills of the Bavarian Alps. She studied architecture in Munich and is currently a research associate in the Department of Architecture at the Technical University of Munich. She also works as a freelance graphic designer, illustrator, and author.

Cornelia Haas has been illustrating childrens' and adolescents' books since 2001. She was born near Augsburg, Germany, in 1972. She studied design at the Münster University of Applied Sciences and is currently a professor on the faculty of Münster University of Applied Sciences teaching illustration.

Marc Robitzky, born in 1973, studied at the Technical School of Art in Hamburg and the Academy of Visual Arts in Frankfurt. He works as a freelance illustrator and communication designer in Aschaffenburg (Germany).

Ulrich Renz was born in Stuttgart, Germany, in 1960. After studying French literature in Paris he graduated from medical school in Lübeck and worked as head of a scientific publishing company. He is now a writer of non-fiction books as well as children's fiction books.

Do you like drawing?

Here are the pictures from the story to color in:

www.sefa-bilingual.com/coloring

www.ingramcontent.com/pod-product-compliance
Lightning Source LLC
LaVergne TN
LVHW070449080526
838202LV00035B/2782